NEW LINES

NEW LINES

An Anthology
edited by
ROBERT CONQUEST

LONDON
MACMILLAN & CO LTD
NEW YORK · ST MARTIN'S PRESS
1957

MACMILLAN AND COMPANY LIMITED
London Bombay Calcutta Madras Melbourne

THE MACMILLAN COMPANY OF CANADA LIMITED
Toronto

ST MARTIN'S PRESS INC
New York

PRINTED IN GREAT BRITAIN

For Tatiana

ACKNOWLEDGEMENTS are due to Fantasy Press for 'Afternoon in Florence', 'The Island' and 'Identity', by Elizabeth Jennings, 'Remembering the 'Thirties' and 'Woodpigeons at Raheny', by Donald Davie, and 'Lerici', by Thom Gunn ; to André Deutsch for the remainder of the poems by Elizabeth Jennings ; to Routledge & Kegan Paul for 'Waiting for the Bus', 'Evening in the Khamsin', 'Baie des Anges, Nice', 'The Laughing Hyena, by Hokusai', 'On the Death of a Child', 'Mid-Mediterranean : September Evening', 'Latin Festival', 'Lost, Stolen or Strayed', by D. J. Enright ; to Secker and Warburg for the remainder of D. J. Enright's poems ; and to the Fantasy Press 'Fantasy Poets' series, the University of Reading School of Art, The Marvell Press, Penguin Books, the B.B.C., *Springtime*, and the following periodicals, in which many of the poems first appeared : *The New Statesman & Nation*, *The Listener*, *The Spectator*, *Tribune*, *Listen*, *Essays in Criticism*, *Departure*, *The New Yorker*, *Poetry* (Chicago), *The London Magazine*, *Encounter* and *The Irish Times*.

CONTENTS

INTRODUCTION

I

In the late 1920s a group of poets were starting to write who were to be the typical poets of the 1930s. Towards the end of the 1930s a group of writers with quite different attitudes began to emerge, who were to dominate the 1940s. Each of these groups was, if not launched, at any rate presented to public fire by anthologies which took up definite positions. It is a notable fact that no anthology of this sort has appeared in this country for more than ten years.

It is in the belief that a general tendency has once again set in, and that a genuine and healthy poetry of the new period has established itself, that this collection has been made.

2

In the 1940s the mistake was made of giving the Id, a sound player on the percussion side under a strict conductor, too much of a say in the doings of the orchestra as a whole. As it turned out, it could only manage the simpler part of melody and rhythm, and was completely out of its depth with harmony and orchestration. This led to a rapid collapse of public taste, from which we have not yet recovered.

In *Texts and Pretexts* Mr. Aldous Huxley once wrote of another art :

'Some people love music, not wisely, but too well. Even among the musically talented and well-educated you will find them. I know several, excellent performers and widely read, whose passion for music is such, that it robs them of their judgement. . . . One can love music gluttonously and voluptuously (and I have known people whose appetite for sweet sounds was positively hoggish), or one can love it with heart, soul and mind, as a complete and fully developed human being.'

He goes on to speak of 'the sort of people whose bowels yearn at the disgusting caterwaulings of Tziganes ; who love to listen to Negroes and Cossacks ; who swoon at the noises of the Hawaiian guitar, the Russian balalaika, the Argentine saw and even the Wurlitzer organ. . . . In other words they are the sort of people who don't really like music.'

This describes, only too clearly, the sort of corruption which has affected the general attitude to poetry in the last decade. There is no need to be quite so puritanical as Huxley. There would be no harm whatever in people indulging themselves in this way, so long as they did not set up these tastes as general criteria. Unfortunately this restriction has not been observed. In this indiscriminating atmosphere other types of vicious taste, too, began to be catered for. The debilitating theory that poetry *must* be metaphorical gained wide acceptance. Poets were encouraged to produce diffuse and sentimental verbiage, or hollow technical pirouettes : praise even went to writers whose verse seemed to have been put together from the snippets in the 'Towards More Picturesque Speech' page of the *Reader's Digest*. Residual nuisances like the Social-realists, the Lallans-mongers, the church-furnishers and the neo-Georgians were able to maintain themselves. In these circumstances it became more plain than is usually the case that without integrity and judgement enough to prevent surrender to subjective moods or social pressures all the technical and emotional gifts are almost worthless.

At any time a great deal of dubious verse is published, and no great harm comes of this since the good and new usually get published too, and almost as easily. Nowadays publication of poetry, particularly in books, but also in magazines, is severely limited. Expenses are high and publishers are naturally inclined to be less lavish, while, on the other hand, for a very long time there was no specialised verse magazine with any serious authority. This constriction has had an unfortunate effect. The good and new, whose publication was formerly a sort of by-product of the publication of material of lesser quality, has suffered, as poems more in accord with the general taste have been all that publishers could afford.

Many of the writers collected here have already wrested reasonable recognition from middleman and public even in these conditions. Some have not yet done so, in spite of considerable achievement. It is remarkable how many of the poets in this book owe their first publication in book or pamphlet form to small presses running off limited editions — Fantasy Press and the University of Reading School of Art — or to the new Marvell Press, and how many of them have still not had larger volumes published.

3

One must, indeed, distinguish between the poetry being written at any period and the dominant poetic atmosphere. The poet is a hardy life-form, and a dozen writers spring to mind at once who continued to produce fine verse through the worst days of the 'forties. The art went wrong to a far lesser extent than its public, amongst whom the most carefully argued protests were simply unable to get a hearing : 'nothing would happen, no one would notice. Objection, reason, proof — all would be swamped in the universal mess', as Mr. Geoffrey Grigson put it. But some poets, too, were deeply affected, and men capable of moving work were encouraged to regard their task simply as one of making an arrangement of images of sex and violence tapped straight from the unconscious (a sort of upper-middle-brow equivalent of the horror-comic), or to evoke without comment the *naïvetés* and nostalgias of childhood.

To combat this trend was not a purely artistic task. When a condition of this sort takes hold it sometimes lasts for decades. The writers remembered later are odd eccentrics — the Kiplings and Hardys. But even such individuals cannot correct a mood : that requires a general tendency, perhaps of lesser talents.

4

It was in the late 1940s and early 1950s that a number of poets began to emerge who have been progressing from different viewpoints to a certain unity of approach, a new and healthy general standpoint.

In one sense, indeed, the standpoint is not new, but merely the restoration of a sound and fruitful attitude to poetry, of the principle that poetry is written by and for the whole man, intellect, emotions, senses and all. But restorations are not repetitions. The atmosphere, the attack, of these poets is as concentratedly contemporary as could be imagined. To be of one's own time is not an important virtue, but it is a necessary one.

If one had briefly to distinguish this poetry of the fifties from its predecessors, I believe the most important general point would be that it submits to no great systems of theoretical constructs nor agglomerations of unconscious commands. It is free from both mystical and logical compulsions and — like modern philosophy — is empirical in its attitude to all that comes. This reverence for the real person or event is, indeed, a part of the general intellectual ambience (in so far as that is not blind or retrogressive) of our time. One might, without stretching matters too far, say that George Orwell with his principle of real, rather than ideological, honesty, exerted, even though indirectly, one of the major influences on modern poetry.

On the more technical side, though of course related to all this, we see refusal to abandon a rational structure and comprehensible language, even when the verse is most highly charged with sensuous or emotional intent.

It will be seen at once that these poets do not have as much in common as they would if they were a group of doctrine-saddled writers forming a definite school complete with programme and rules. What they do have in common is perhaps, at its lowest, little more than a negative determination to avoid bad principles. By itself that cannot guarantee good poetry. Still, it is a good deal, and the fact that such agreement has been reached from various starting-points and by the discipline of practice, rather than by the acceptance of *a priori* dogmas, is a point in favour of its depth and soundness.

When Coleridge wrote, 'poetry is the blossom and the fragrancy of all human knowledge, human thoughts, human passions, emotions, language', he was expressing the central tradition of all English poetry, classical or romantic. Only in occasional aberrations have attempts been made to delete everything but the emotion, attempts which naturally petered out into sentimentalism. But Coleridge also makes a striking point when he counts 'language', too, not simply as a vehicle, but among the other main bases of verse. Post-war poetry has often been criticised for dealing too much with language, and with the poetic process itself, as though these were in some way illegitimate subjects. This seems rather a superficial misconception : the nature of art and of the whole problem of communication has in recent years been seen to be at the centre of philosophy and of human life, and perhaps no subject is potentially more fruitful — so long, indeed, as any tendency to write about syntactic and semantic problems in isolation from their significance and content is avoided.

5

The most glaring fault awaiting correction when the new period opened was the omission of the necessary intellectual component from poetry. It cannot be denied that this has led, to some extent, to a tendency to over-intellectualise. Some years ago Mr. John Wain advocated the methods of Mr William Empson in poetry. Other writers revived eighteenth-century forms. And soon a number of young poets were following Empsonian and similar academic principles and often producing verse of notable aridity. As a starting-point for Mr. Wain and others this was a not unreasonable way of learning the first lesson — that a poem needs an intellectual backbone. But that it became merely a fashionable formula among the young is unfortunate. Intellectual frameworks can be filled out with bad materials as well as good, and Empsonianism has been almost as much a vehicle for unpleasant exhibitionism and sentimentality as the trends it was designed to correct. The second lesson, that an intellectual skeleton is not worth much unless it is given the flesh of humanity, irony, passion or sanity, was not always learnt.

This is perhaps only to say that any forthright lead will find its followers and imitators among young writers. And at least the Empsonian fashion is an improvement on its predecessors — in reading the poorer five-finger exercises one is always consoled by the thought of how much worse they used to be when other less restrained styles were in vogue.

Still it is noticeable that the writings of that group are admirable almost exactly in inverse ratio to their reliance on formulae. (Mr. Amis is a notable example. And his 'The Voice of Authority'[1] is both a sample of the method at its best and a conscious satire on it.)

6

The connoisseur of influences would probably find that the general recognition of Yeats as the great poet of the century is reflected in a considerable debt of matter and method among the poets in this book. Writers such as Robert Graves and Edwin Muir also have their echoes. It is a question not merely of technical influence, but of the example of these poets' unabashed and untheoretical eye to visual and emotional events, which their sometimes eccentric views cannot obscure. Auden, too, casts an obvious shadow here and there : who can escape that large and rational talent ? But, in his case, it is mainly a matter of technical

[1] I am told that this poem may not be clear to overseas readers; it should be explained that 'O'Grady says' is a game practised in army physical training for its supposed use in sharpening the wits. The class is expected to obey commands only when these are prefaced by the words 'O'Grady says' : ordinary orders must be ignored.

influence. There is little of the Auden tendency to turn abstractions into beings in their own right.

7

This book confines itself to poets who found themselves not earlier than the late 1940s and whose first books have been published since the war, and in most cases in the 1950s.

The nine poets given (eight of whom are not, any more than the publishers, responsible for any of the views expressed here) are not the only ones who might have been selected to represent present trends. They are all, however, writers with a reasonable body of work behind them. Bulk is not itself a virtue, yet it seemed best to rest the case on this solid evidence, and not include the other, mainly younger, talents which have clearly begun to emerge.

It is easier to compose ambitious generalisations about the nature of poetry today than to write the actual poems. The stage needed sweeping : but now let them speak for themselves.

Elizabeth Jennings

AFTERNOON IN FLORENCE

THIS afternoon disturbs within the mind
No other afternoon, is out of time
Yet lies within a definite sun to end
In night that is in time.   Yet hold it here
Our eyes, our minds, to make the city clear.

Light detains no prisoner here at all
In brick or stone but sends a freedom out,
Extends a shadow like a deeper thought,
Makes churches move, once still,
Rocking in light as music rocks the bell.

So eyes make room for light and minds make
  room
For image of the city tangible.
We look down on the city and a dream
Opens to wakefulness, and waking on
This peace perpetuates this afternoon.

THE ISLAND

ALL travellers escape the mainland here.
The same geology torn from the stretch

Of hostile homelands is a head of calm,
And the same sea that pounds a foreign beach
Turns strangers here familiar, looses them
Kindly as pebbles shuffled up the shore.

Each brings an island in his heart to square
With what he finds, and all is something strange
But most expected.   In this innocent air
Thoughts can assume a meaning, island strength
Is outward, inward, each man measures it,
Unrolls his happiness a shining length.

And this awareness grows upon itself,
Fastens on minds, is forward, backward, here.
The island focuses escape and free
Men on the shore are also islands, steer
Self to knowledge of self in the calm sea,
Seekers who are their own discovery.

IDENTITY

WHEN I decide I shall assemble you
Or, more precisely, when I decide which thoughts
Of mine about you fit most easily together,
Then I can learn what I have loved, what lets
Light through the mind.   The residue
Of what you may be goes.   I gather

Only as lovers or friends gather at all,
For making friends means this —
Image and passion combined into a whole
Pattern within the loving mind, not her or his

2

Concurring there.   You can project the full
Picture of lover or friend that is not either.

So then assemble me,
Your exact picture firm and credible,
Though as I think myself I may be free
And accurate enough.
That you love what is truthful to your will
Is all that ever can be answered for
And, what is more,
Is all we make each other when we love.

MUSIC AND WORDS

No human singing can
    Express itself without
Words that usurp the sounds
    That pour forth from the throat.
But when the music ends
    There lie within our minds
Thoughts that refuse to fit,
    That will not sing or scan
Or alter what they mean.

Yet we believe in song
    Some meaning that no word
Can catch is finely caught,
    That music is a state
Where truth is overheard.
    But we are wrong, are wrong :
Thoughts still are shaped of hard
    Unalterable stuff
We think we can forget
    If we sing loud enough.

3

Now watch this autumn that arrives
In smells. All looks like summer still ;
Colours are quite unchanged, the air
On green and white serenely thrives.
Heavy the trees with growth and full
The fields. Flowers flourish everywhere.

Proust who collected time within
A child's cake would understand
The ambiguity of this —
Summer still raging while a thin
Column of smoke stirs from the land
Proving that autumn gropes for us.

But every season is a kind
Of rich nostalgia. We give names —
Autumn and summer, winter, spring —
As though to unfasten from the mind
Our moods and give them outward forms.
We want the certain, solid thing.

But I am carried back against
My will into a childhood where
Autumn is bonfires, marbles, smoke ;
I lean against my window, fenced
From evocations in the air.
When I said autumn, autumn broke.

FLORENCE: DESIGN FOR A CITY

Take one bowl, one valley
Assisted by hills to peace

And let the hills hold back the wind a little
Only turning the trees
Only dividing the shadows
With a simple movement of sun
Across the valley's face.

And then set cypresses up,
So dark they seem to contain their repeated shadows
In a straight and upward leap,
So dark that the sun seems to avoid them to show
How austere they are, stiff, admonishing gestures
Towards the city, yet also protective
To the deep houses that the sun makes more deep.

Here I say the mind is open, is freed ;
Anchored only to frailest thoughts, we are
Triumphantly subdued to the light's full glare.
It is simple then to be a stranger,
To have a mind that is wide
To permit the city to settle between our thoughts,
As between those hills, and flower and glow inside.

NOT IN THE GUIDE-BOOKS

NOBODY stays here long ;
    Deliberate visitors know
There is nothing here the guide-books show,
    No ruin or statue to sustain
Some great emotion in their stone.
    So visitors soon go.

Some travellers stay a little
    To collect wine or corn
And here breathe in the over-subtle

Smell of places worn
Not by a marvellous death or battle
    But by their insignificance brought down.

Yet good, a place like this,
    For one grown tired of histories
To shape a human myth,
    A story but for his
Delight, where he might make the place
    His own success
Building what no one else had bothered with —
    A simple life or death.

A WAY OF LOOKING

IT is the association after all
We seek, we would retrace our thoughts to find
The thought of which this landscape is the image,
Then pay the thought and not the landscape
    homage.
It is as if the tree and waterfall
Had their first roots and source within the mind.

But something plays a trick upon the scene :
A different kind of light, a stranger colour
Flows down on the appropriated view.
Nothing within the mind fits. This is new.
Thought and reflection must begin again
To fit the image and to make it true.

PIAZZA SAN MARCO

HERE if you seek philosophies you find
Your usual clear-cut notions have been dulled.

Your thoughts will bask among reflections and
Cerebral definitions will be filled
With tangible adornment. Be all eye,

Watch how the campanile masks the sky
Yet gives you much more hope of sun behind,
See how the horses gallop silently
And to no end. Set firmer thinking by.

Water and stone are all that you can use
As metaphors.
Kings in other times built structures which
Could bear caprice of sculptors, but you have
Only thin thoughts, no faith that you can touch.
There is so much
That separates those motionless proud horses
From minds that only move through words,
      through verses.

IN THE NIGHT

OUT of my window late at night I gape
And see the stars but do not watch them really,
And hear the trains but do not listen clearly ;
Inside my mind I turn about to keep
Myself awake, yet am not there entirely.
Something of me is out in the dark landscape.

How much am I then what I think, how much what
      I feel ?
How much the eye that seems to keep stars straight ?
Do I control what I can contemplate
Or is it my vision that's amenable ?

7

I turn in my mind, my mind is a room whose wall
I can see the top of but never completely scale.

All that I love is, like the night, outside,
Good to be gazed at, looking as if it could
With a simple gesture be brought inside my head
Or in my heart, but my thoughts about it divide
Me from my object. Now deep in my bed
I turn and the world turns on the other side.

John Holloway

THE CONFLUENCE

HE and she make an ocean
Of all complexity :
When not the lightest motion
Troubles the upper sea,
Stingray and squid and decapod
Quarter the still uncharted bed.

And when a breeze may ruffle
The water white, or black,
Or passing steamer shuffle
Its wake across its back,
Nothing at all disturbs the deep
Where their blind monsters drift and sleep.

Wisely, they only cruise
Up on the surface here,
Not incontinently use
Plummet and bathysphere :
The waters mix, they need not ask
Rashly what draws them to their task.

EPITAPH FOR A MAN

TAKE notice. This neglected stone bears no request
(Stranger, friend, passer-by)

9

To read. It carries an inscription lest
    Merely from curiosity
    You should. A kind of riddle lies
Here. Or will do . . . His life made barely sense,
    Having no virtues, and but one vice :
A substance shorn of nearly all its accidents.

That one was cosmic though. It took in all the lot.
        Being a capacity
    To say, do, think, preach, trust in what was not
        In everything. Half-lie and lie
        All round the clock : until he blacked
    His shadows' shadow to a neat design
        That all and sundry took for fact.
(Why look, as black as cherries : as white as wine.)

Deep crimson and clear gold, and every proper tint,
        Made him uncomfortable.
    He settled for the morning dress of print.
        Yet even this could give him trouble
        Run off by others. He was prone
    To deem all strangers' flowers poisonous ;
        And yet he (if it was his own)
Could glimpse a matchless charger in a chocolate mouse.

Really no moral point attaches to this tale :
        What a complex task
    It would be to extract one, and what could it avail ?
        One question, though, it's right to ask,
        Or, at the least, hint tactfully :
    Are you aware of what both of us are,
        And therefore whose this place must be . . . ?
Perhaps it was imprudent to have read, to write, so far.

THE MINUTE

WALKING across a world and map,
Panting from having climbed the cliff
When a blue field's one dazzling flower
Made a gold day, no wonder if
The hidden inner weir should snap
And loose its strong long-hoarded power
All in a flash : as if the sharp
Grid of his map turned wire, and poured
Music out of one single harp
Where all the strings could ring one chord.

Half lost in dust-dry bracken : then
Up from the mind's deep middle jet,
Clear as a bird, the sudden gleam
Shot like a double day ; and yet
He scarcely saw the moment when
The gentle current's crystal stream
Turned ice turned diamond and took light
And stole the secret of the sun
To fuse and flare and make one bright
Minute : and then the thing was done.

ELEGY FOR AN ESTRANGEMENT

ONE had grown almost affluent. One had
Almost deliberately chosen to be poor.
Each of them knew the other's choice was bad,
And, at the same time, each became unsure.
    They grew less intimate than before.
        Yet both had once known pain
And much bewilderment, that no overt act

Could quite convey the intimacy they felt.
And then, had been bewildered over again
To find this as true with women, as with men.

For one, that find was a vague flaw ; whereby
The act he coveted might just be dulled
A trifle. But if he ignored it confidently
The two-backed beast could still turn hollow gold
    And he grasp all its vault might hold.
        But for the other one
It was a plain enigma ; that he thought
About until it had perplexed him quite :
He being forced to spend much time alone,
And evaluate many more things than he had done.

It was before this time that they had walked
Together home from school : seen scaffolds grow
Like bamboos down long modern streets, and talked
Of how they both would make the future go
    Into a pattern fine to show ;
        Or strolled on holidays
Over the dip-slope and chill showery rim
Down to the villages planting out the plain,
Where the quiet chalk, at last, a hundred ways,
Gives tongue, and globes the streams with mimulus.

Later, around a College 'quad, they spoke
Of subtler things : and understood them well
One preferred Aristotle or blunt Locke,
And one, Spinoza's calm unlikely tale :
    But none of these could half reveal
        To either one of them
How by some gentle yet insistent art
To amalgam things that now trended apart ;

Or how unlikely it was, any golden stream
Would gush from the wilder uplands not of place, but
    time.

Time by its formal definition moves
To a sidereal or a solar rhythm
Too big to watch : perplexed among its grooves
Each tried to fashion and perfect his system,
    And both drew slowly to them
        Whatever they could find
(Like pieces for a puzzle) to complete
The equilibrium of the closed circuit.
The few inter-connexions that remained
Troubling them less . . . as they grew more purblind.

Theirs was the typical case : not in one night,
But over years, as their great scheme, each tried,
Like a bold landscape-gardener, to create
A whole new Nature, calm and rectified.
    And each one watched his dream subside.
        Yet never saw the change,
For by enharmony, dream and act were blent :
Or seemed to be so, as their sense grew blunt.
The fragments, though, grew harder to arrange.
They could not be so intimate. It was strange.

And then they sealed the rock : heretical
When least they glimpsed it. Each of them contrived
To ignore the little tinkling passing bell.
The god expired too slow to be revived.
    Yet even so he was short-lived,
        And thus they knew much pain :
Weeds choked the garden, the diagrams all turned
Into grey scribbles. Hollow gold all spent.

A flowerless river skulking through a plain.
Streets of an endless town.   Night falls in rain.

TOPER'S POEM

Now I deliver this curse : —
What is lost for good,
No one shall ever find.
Blind shall lead blind.
No child shall have food
Unless it suck its nurse.
All broken things shall be
Broken three times three.
And this curse I deliver
As I snooze in clover
With sun hot down on me.

Next I pronounce a blessing : —
There shall be a new birth :
Bad men be quite forgiven,
Happy men packed off to Heaven,
Saints be kept on Earth,
And all (their sins confessing)
Think they can sin much more
Virtuously than before.
This blessing I utter
As I slump down in the gutter
Before my own front door.

Last, I prophesy : —
All rough things and all smooth
Shall be twinned and wed,
And share one single bed,

And this is simple truth
Plain to half an eye :
In this turn-table land
Crazy curse, and
Monstrous benediction
And this monstrous pre-diction,
One and all, stand.

THE SHELL

THIS is the shell. Time out of mind,
That shy, reserved old man
Treasured it on his shelf ; all spined
And horned, a harsh white saurian.
But through its cave a low
Chant seemed to float : a curious find,
Crabbed as a bird's claw, calm as snow.

I was not there, I did not hear
The clang of the one bell ;
But if I lift my hand, my ear
Breathes a smooth music from the shell
He gave me. Breathes the small
Chord it intones all day ; queer,
Aloof, almost ironical.

At that great age, when the heart's beat
May halt as easily
As a light footstep in a street
And sense no pain, I think that he
Had no grief, no alarm :
But turned towards his new retreat
Quiet as his shell, and twice as calm.

AT the first hour from dawn
The traveller in the window seat
Rubbed his eyes, woke from a daze,
Brushed his rough hair back with great
Podgy fingers, gave a yawn,
Cleared the pane's white dewy haze,
Then stared so eagerly, it might
Have been his home place come in sight.

But at the second hour from dawn
The traveller in the window seat
Suddenly turned away from the world
As though he saw some thing too sweet
Or too bitter to be borne ;
And when he met my glance, he curled
His body to the wall, and wept
I thought ; but it may be he slept.

At the third hour from dawn
The ticket man rolled back the door :
The traveller blurted out that he
Wanted another ticket for
Some other place, somewhere further on ;
He spoke shortly, confusedly ;
But I saw he did not know,
Now, where in the world to go.

WARNING TO A GUEST

AGAINST the flare and descant of the gas
I heard an old woman in a shop maintain
This fog comes when the moon is on the wane :
And ten full days must pass

16

Before the crescent mows it in like grass.
   Shun the black puddles, the scrub hedge
Down to the sea. Keep to the wet streets where
Mercury and sodium flood their sullen fire.
Tonight, do not disturb the water's edge.

There'll be no storm, I know : having often gone,
In storm or calm, where the strong tide has flowed
Right to the tunnel underneath the road
    Along the formless dune.
But this is the third quarter of the moon
  In fog. There'll be no drench and roar
Of breakers : the quiet tide will drift
Idly among the pebbles, and then sift
Back to the sea. Yet shun that dark foreshore.

There'll be no sound : except the echoing
Horn of a baffled ship, shut out from home,
And the small birds that skirt the stranded foam.
    Dunlin and sanderling
Feed through the night, or lightly they take wing
  Down the soft fog. So sharp their pulse
Trills, and their dram of blood burns up so clear,
Each minute, in their bright sight, makes a year.
But you may catch the note of something else.

I have watched you, as you have visited at this house,
And know, from knowing myself, that you will be
Quick to people the shore, the fog, the sea,
    With all the fabulous
Things of the moon's dark side. No, stay with us.
  Do not demand a walk tonight
Down to the sea. It makes no place for those
Like you and me who, to sustain our pose,
Need wine and conversation, colour and light.

Philip Larkin

MAIDEN NAME

MARRYING left your maiden name disused.
Its five light sounds no longer mean your face,
Your voice, your sudden variants of grace ;
For since you were so thankfully confused
By law with someone else, you cannot be
Semantically the same as that young beauty :
It was of her that these two words were used.

Now it's a phrase, applicable to no one,
Lying just where you left it, scattered through
Old lists, old programmes, a school prize or two,
Packets of letters tied with tartan ribbon —
Then is it scentless, weightless, strengthless, wholly
Untruthful ? Try whispering it slowly.
No, it means you. Or, since you're past and gone,

It means what we feel now about you then —
How beautiful you were, and near, and young,
So vivid, you might still be there among
Those first few days, unfingermarked again.
So your old name shelters our faithfulness,
Instead of losing shape and meaning less
With your depreciating luggage laden.

ONCE I am sure there's nothing going on
I step inside, letting the door thud shut.
Another church : matting, seats, and stone,
And little books ; sprawlings of flowers, cut
For Sunday, brownish now ; some brass and stuff
Up at the holy end ; the small neat organ ;
And a tense, musty, unignorable silence,
Brewed God knows how long.   Hatless, I take off
My cycle-clips in awkward reverence,

Move forward, run my hand around the font.
From where I stand, the roof looks almost new —
Cleaned, or restored ? Someone would know : I
    don't.
Mounting the lectern, I peruse a few
Hectoring large-scale verses, and pronounce
'Here endeth' much more loudly than I'd meant.
The echoes snigger briefly.   Back at the door
I sign the book, donate an Irish sixpence,
Reflect the place was not worth stopping for.

Yet stop I did : in fact I often do,
And always end much at a loss like this,
Wondering what to look for ; wondering, too,
When churches fall completely out of use
What we shall turn them into, if we shall keep
A few cathedrals chronically on show,
Their parchment, plate and pyx in locked cases,
Letting the rest rent-free to rain and sheep.
Shall we avoid them as unlucky places ?

Or, after dark, will dubious women come
To make their children touch a particular stone ;

Pick simples for a cancer ; or on some
Advised night see walking a dead one ?
Power of some sort or other will go on
In games, in riddles, seemingly at random ;
But superstition, like belief, must die,
And what remains when disbelief has gone ?
Grass, weedy pavement, brambles, buttress, sky,

A shape less recognisable each week,
A purpose more obscure. I wonder who
Will be the last, the very last, to seek
This place for what it was ; one of the crew
Who tap and jot and know what roodlofts were ?
Some ruin-bibber, randy for antique,
Or Christmas-addict, counting on a whiff
Of gown-and-bands and organ-pipes and myrrh ?
Or will he be my representative,

Bored, uninformed, knowing the ghostly silt
Dispersed, yet tending to this cross of ground
Through suburb scrub because it held unspilt
So long and equably what since is found
Only in separation — marriage, and birth,
And death, and thoughts of these — round which was
        built
This special shell ? For, though I've no idea
What this accoutred frowsty barn is worth,
It pleases me to stand in silence here ;

A serious house on serious earth it is,
In whose blent air all our compulsions rest,
Are recognised, and robed as destinies.
And that much never can be obsolete,
Since someone will for ever be surprising

A hunger in himself to be more serious,
And gravitating with it to this ground,
Which, he once heard, was proper to grow wise in,
If only that so many dead lie round.

I REMEMBER, I REMEMBER

COMING up England by a different line
For once, early in the cold new year,
We stopped, and, watching men with number-plates
Sprint down the platform to familiar gates,
'Why, Coventry!' I exclaimed. 'I was born here.'

I leant far out, and squinnied for a sign
That this was still the town that had been 'mine'
So long, but found I wasn't even clear
Which side was which. From where those cycle-
        crates
Were standing, had we annually departed

For all those family hols? . . . A whistle went:
Things moved. I sat back, staring at my boots.
'Was that,' my friend smiled, 'where you "have your
        roots"?'
No, only where my childhood was unspent,
I wanted to retort, just where I started:

By now I've got the whole place clearly charted.
Our garden, first; where I did not invent
Blinding theologies of flowers and fruits,
And wasn't spoken to by an old hat.
And here we have that splendid family

I never ran to when I got depressed,
The boys all biceps and the girls all chest,
Their comic Ford, their farm where I could be
'Really myself'. I'll show you, come to that,
The bracken where I never trembling sat,

Determined to go through with it ; where she
Lay back, and 'all became a burning mist'.
And, in those offices, my doggerel
Was not set up in blunt ten-point, nor read
By a distinguished cousin of the Mayor,

Who didn't call and tell my father : *There
Before us, if we could but see ahead —*
'You look as if you wished the place in Hell,'
My friend said, 'judging from your face.' 'Oh well,
I suppose it's not the place's fault,' I said.

'Nothing, like something, happens anywhere.'

SKIN

OBEDIENT daily dress,
You cannot always keep
That unfakable young surface.
You must learn your lines —
Anger, amusement, sleep ;
Those few forbidding signs

Of the continuous coarse
Sand-laden wind, time ;
You must thicken, work loose
Into an old bag

Carrying a soiled name.
Parch then ; be roughened ; sag ;

And pardon me, that I
Could find, when you were new,
No brash festivity
To wear you at, such as
Clothes are entitled to
Till the fashion changes.

LATEST FACE

LATEST face, so effortless
Your great arrival at my eyes,
No one standing near could guess
Your beauty had no home till then ;
Precious vagrant, recognise
My look, and do not turn again.

Admirer and admired embrace
On a useless level where
I contain your current grace,
You my judgement ; yet to move
Into real untidy air
Brings no lasting attribute —
Bargains, suffering, and love,
Not this always-planned salute.

Lies grow dark around us : will
The statue of your beauty walk ?
Must I wade behind it, till
Something's found — or is not found —
Far too late for turning back ?

Or, if I will not shift my ground,
Is your power actual — can
Denial of you duck and run,
Stay out of sight and double round,
Leap from the sun with mask and brand
And murder and not understand ?

BORN YESTERDAY
(FOR SALLY AMIS)

TIGHTLY-folded bud,
I have wished you something
None of the others would :
Not the usual stuff
About being beautiful,
Or running off a spring
Of innocence or love —
They will all wish you that,
And should it prove possible,
Well, you're a lucky girl.

But if it shouldn't, then
May you be ordinary ;
Have like other women
An average of talents :
Not ugly, not good-looking,
Nothing uncustomary
To pull you off your balance,
That, unworkable itself,
Stops all the rest from working.
In fact, may you be dull —
If that is what a skilled,
Vigilant, flexible,

Unemphasised, enthralled
Catching of happiness is called.

TRIPLE TIME

THIS empty street, this sky to blandness scoured,
This air, a little indistinct with autumn
Like a reflection, constitute the present —
A time traditionally soured,
A time unrecommended by event.

But equally they make up something else :
This is the future furthest childhood saw
Between long houses, under travelling skies,
Heard in contending bells —
An air lambent with adult enterprise,

And on another day will be the past,
A valley cropped by fat neglected chances
That we insensately forbore to fleece.
On this we blame our last
Threadbare perspectives, seasonal decrease.

TOADS

WHY should I let the toad *work*
    Squat on my life ?
Can't I use my wit as a pitchfork
    And drive the brute off ?

Six days of the week it soils
    With its sickening poison —

Just for paying a few bills !
  That's out of proportion.

Lots of folk live on their wits :
  Lecturers, lispers,
Losels, loblolly-men, louts —
  They don't end as paupers.

Lots of folk live up lanes
  With a fire in a bucket ;
Eat windfalls and tinned sardines —
  They seem to like it.

Their nippers have got bare feet,
  Their unspeakable wives
Are skinny as whippets — and yet
  No one actually *starves*.

Ah, were I courageous enough
  To shout *Stuff your pension !*
But I know, all too well, that's the stuff
  That dreams are made on :

For something sufficiently toad-like
  Squats in me too ;
Its hunkers are heavy as hard luck,
  And cold as snow,

And will never allow me to blarney
  My way to getting
The fame and the girl and the money
  All at one sitting.

I don't say, one bodies the other
  One's spiritual truth ;

But I do say it's hard to lose either,
   When you have both.

LINES ON A YOUNG LADY'S
PHOTOGRAPH ALBUM

AT last you yielded up the album, which,
Once open, sent me distracted.   All your ages
Matt and glossy on the thick black pages !
Too much confectionery, too rich :
I choke on such nutritious images.

My swivel eye hungers from pose to pose —
In pigtails, clutching a reluctant cat ;
Or furred yourself, a sweet girl-graduate ;
Or lifting a heavy-headed rose
Beneath a trellis, or in a trilby hat

(Faintly disturbing, that, in several ways) —
From every side you strike at my control,
Not least through these disquieting chaps who loll
At ease about your earlier days :
Not quite your class, I'd say, dear, on the whole.

But O, photography ! as no art is,
Faithful and disappointing ! that records
Dull days as dull, and hold-it smiles as frauds,
And will not censor blemishes
Like washing-lines, and Hall's-Distemper boards,

But shows the cat as disinclined, and shades
A chin as doubled when it is, what grace
Your candour thus confers upon her face !

How overwhelmingly persuades
That this is a real girl in a real place,

In every sense empirically true !
Or is it just *the past* ? Those flowers, that gate,
These misty parks and motors, lacerate
Simply by being over ; you
Contract my heart by looking out of date.

Yes, true ; but in the end, surely, we cry
Not only at exclusion, but because
It leaves us free to cry. We know *what was*
Won't call on us to justify
Our grief, however hard we yowl across

The gap from eye to page. So I am left
To mourn (without a chance of consequence)
You, balanced on a bike against a fence ;
To wonder if you'd spot the theft
Of this one of you bathing ; to condense,

In short, a past that no one now can share,
No matter whose your future ; calm and dry,
It holds you like a heaven, and you lie
Unvariably lovely there,
Smaller and clearer as the years go by.

Thom Gunn

LERICI

SHELLEY was drowned near here. Arms at his side
He fell submissive through the waves, and he
Was but a minor conquest of the sea :
The darkness that he met was nurse not bride.

Others make gestures with arms open wide,
Compressing in the minute before death
What great expense of muscle and of breath
They would have made if they had never died.

Byron was worth the sea's pursuit. His touch
Was masterful to water, audience
To which he could react until an end.
Strong swimmers, fishermen, explorers : such
Dignify death by thriftless violence —
Squandering with so little left to spend.

ON THE MOVE
'Man, you gotta Go.'

THE blue jay scuffling in the bushes follows
Some hidden purpose, and the gust of birds

That spurts across the field, the wheeling swallows,
Have nested in the trees and undergrowth.
Seeking their instinct, or their poise, or both,
One moves with an uncertain violence
Under the dust thrown by a baffled sense
Or the dull thunder of approximate words.

On motorcycles, up the road, they come :
Small, black, as flies hanging in heat, the Boys,
Until the distance throws them forth, their hum
Bulges to thunder held by calf and thigh.
In goggles, donned impersonality,
In gleaming jackets trophied with the dust,
They strap in doubt — by hiding it, robust —
And almost hear a meaning in their noise.

Exact conclusion of their hardiness
Has no shape yet, but from known whereabouts
They ride, direction where the tyres press.
They scare a flight of birds across the field :
Much that is natural, to the will must yield.
Men manufacture both machine and soul,
And use what they imperfectly control
To dare a future from the taken routes.

It is a part solution, after all.
One is not necessarily discord
On earth ; or damned because, half animal,
One lacks direct instinct, because one wakes
Afloat on movement that divides and breaks.
One joins the movement in a valueless world,
Choosing it, till, both hurler and the hurled,
One moves as well, always toward, toward.

A minute holds them, who have come to go :
The self-defined, astride the created will
They burst away ; the towns they travel through
Are home for neither bird nor holiness,
For birds and saints complete their purposes.
At worst, one is in motion; and at best,
Reaching no absolute, in which to rest,
One is always nearer by not keeping still.

California

HUMAN CONDITION

Now it is fog, I walk
Contained within my coat ;
No castle more cut off
By reason of its moat :
Only the sentry's cough,
The mercenaries' talk.

The street lamps, visible,
Drop no light on the ground,
But press beams painfully
In a yard of fog around.
I am condemned to be
An individual.

In the established border
There balances a mere
Pinpoint of consciousness.
I stay, or start from, here :
No fog makes more or less
The neighbouring disorder.

Particular, I must
Find out the limitation
Of mind and universe,
To pick thought and sensation
And turn to my own use
Disordered hate or lust.

I seek, to break, my span.
I am my one touchstone.
This is a test more hard
Than any ever known.
And thus I keep my guard
On that which makes me man.

Much is unknowable.
No problem shall be faced
Until the problem is ;
I, born to fog, to waste,
Walk through hypothesis,
An individual.

MERLIN IN THE CAVE: HE SPECULATES
WITHOUT A BOOK

THIS was the end and yet, another start :
Held by the arms of lust from lust I pace
About the dim fulfilment of my art,
Impatient in the flesh I eye a space
Where, warlock, once I might have left this place,
A form of life my tool, creeping across
The shelving rock as rank convolvulus.

The Rock. The space, too narrow for a hand.
Pressing my head between two slopes of stone

I peer at what I do not understand,
The movement : clouds, and separate rooks blown
Back on their flight.   Where do they fly, alone ?
I lost their instinct. It was late. To me
The bird is only meat for augury.

And here the mauve convolvulus falls in,
Its narrow stalk as fat and rich in sap
As I was rich in lusting to begin
A life I could have had and finished up
Years, years before. With aphrodisiac
I brought back vigour ; oiled and curled my hair ;
Reduced my huge obesity, to wear

The green as tightly girdled at my waist
As any boy who leapt about the court ;
And with an unguent I made my chest
Fit for the iron plate. I still held short
Of wrestling as the boys did : from their sport
They slid back panting on the tiles to look
At one distinguished now by scent, not book.

Love was a test : I was all-powerful,
So failed, because I let no fault intrude.
A philosophic appetite. By rule
I calculated each fond attitude
But those that self-distrust makes more than mood,
The quick illogical motions, negative
But evidence that lovers move and live.

I watch the flux I never guessed : the grass ;
The watchful animal that gnaws a root,
Knowing possession means the risk of loss ;
Ripeness that rests an hour in the fruit.

Yet locked here with the very absolute
I challenged, I must try to break the hold :
This cave is empty, and is very cold.

I must grow back through knowledge, passing it
Like casual landmarks in a well-known land,
Great mausoleums over ancient wit,
Doors that would swing at my complacent hand ;
And come at last, being glad to understand
The touched, the seen, and only those, to where
I find the earth is suddenly black and near.

And having reached the point where there remain
No knacks or habits, and these empty cells
Are matched by a great emptiness in my brain :
Unhampered by remembered syllables,
The youth I wasted at precocious spells
Will grow upon me, and my wants agree
In the sweet promiscuity of the bee.

And yet, the danger. All within my mind
Hovers complete, and if it never grows
It never rots ; for what I leave behind
Contains no fight within itself : the rose
Is full and drops no petal, emblems doze
Perfect and quiet as if engraved in books,
Not like the fighting boys and wind-torn rooks.

The bee's world and the rook's world are the same :
Where clouds do, or do not, let through the light ;
Too mixed, unsimple, for a simple blame ;
Belligerent : but no one starts the fight,
And nothing ends it but a storm or night.

Alchemists, only, boil away the pain,
And pick out value as one small dry grain.

And turned upon the flooding relative,
What could I do but start the quest once more
Towards the terrible cave in which I live,
The absolute prison where chance thrust me before
I built it round me on my study floor ;
What could I do but seek the synthesis
As each man does, of what his nature is ?

Knowing the end to movement, I will shrink
From movement not for its own wilful sake.
— How can a man live, and not act or think
Without an end ? But I must act, and make
The meaning in each movement that I take.
Rook, bee, you are the whole and not a part.
This is an end, and yet another start.

AUTUMN CHAPTER IN A NOVEL

THROUGH woods, Madame Une Telle, a trifle ill
With idleness, but no less beautiful,
Walks with the young tutor, round their feet
Mob syllables slurred to a fine complaint,
Which in their time held off the natural heat.

The sun is distant, and they fill out space
Sweatless as watercolour under glass.
He kicks abruptly. But we may suppose
The leaves he scatters thus will settle back
In much the same position as they rose.

A tutor's indignation works on air,
Altering nothing ; action bustles where,
Towards the pool by which they lately stood,
The husband comes discussing with his bailiff
Poachers, the broken fences round the wood.

Pighead ! The poacher is at large, and lingers,
A dead mouse gripped between his sensitive fingers :
Fences already keep the live game out :
See how your property twists her parasol,
Hesitates in the tender trap of doubt.

Here they repair, here daily handle lightly
The brief excitements that disturb them nightly ;
Sap draws back inch by inch, and to the ground
The words they uttered rustle constantly :
Silent, they watch the growing, weightless mound.

They leave at last a chosen element,
Resume the motions of their discontent ;
She takes her sewing up, and he again
Names to her son the deserts on the globe,
And leaves thrust violently upon the pane.

A PLAN OF SELF-SUBJECTION

A FRAGMENT of weak flesh that circles round
Between the sky and the hot crust of hell
I circle because I have found
That magic circles are a useful spell
Against contentment, which comes on by stealth,
Because I have found that from the heaven sun
Can scorch like hell itself,
I end my circle where I had begun.

I put this pen to paper and my verse
Imposes order on my fault described
So that my fault is worse —
Not from condonement but that, double dyed
To rot, it should be treated as the strong,
Obscured with clearness, metaphysical mist,
Yet before very long
From poem back to original I twist.

As Alexander or Mark Antony
Or Coriolanus, whom I most admire,
I mask self-flattery.
And yet however much I may aspire
I stay myself — no perfect king or lover
Or stoic. Even this becomes unreal.
Each tainted with the other
Becomes diseased, both self and self's ideal.

In sex do I not dither more than either
In verse or pose, does not the turncoat sense
Show itself slicker, lither
In changing sides according to the hints
That hopes give out, or action seems to breathe ?
Here is most shade my longing, from the sun
And that hot hell beneath.
My circle's end is where I have begun.

PUSS IN BOOTS TO THE GIANT

IN fine simplicity
I cry On either side
Far as the eye can see
These fields as green as wide
Are my master's property.

The cattle browse their fill,
All day the tall boys sweat
With the bags in the mill,
And after sun set
Jack has his Jill.

And then upon the grass
How lasting and how clean
Without token alas,
They banish the lean
Highway beggars that pass.

It is not selfishness,
But when they enjoy
Two.triumphs in one place
Every girl and boy
Like the defeated less.

So praise the pitiless, hot
In each other's arms.
Gigglers, gossips, do not
Come near.   You, Itching Palms,
We condemn to Thought.

In fine simplicity
I cry On either side
Far as the eye can see
These fields as green as wide
Are my master's property.

THE INHERITED ESTATE
(to an American in Europe)

A MANSION, string of cottages, a farm,
Before you reach the last black timbered barn

And set your foot upon the path that leads
Up to the hill where Follies and façades
— Typical products of intelligence
That lacks brute purpose — split, disintegrate,
    And, falling with their own rich weight,
Litter the slopes, a record of expense.

So generations of the reckless dead
Put up the ruins you inherited,
And generations of ganged village boys
Have used as fort and ammunition those
Droppings of fashion you explore today.
What country boys and gentlemen have left
        Now smells of green, the fat dark drift
Where the weed's impulse couples with decay.

Is comfort so impermanently built,
A summer-house with blurring fungus spilt
At random on the leaning walls ? is time
Only a carved head that you fish from slime
That winks with muddied eyeball ? does the crash
Of failing stonework sound for all desires ?
    For, once the dilettante tires,
The ornaments he raises fall in trash.

A calm discrimination marks your hate :
Once you inherited the wide estate
The Follies like the land and farm were yours.
Distance has flattered them, for from the moors
The fronts resembled solid palaces :
And though you are not so trusting to believe
    That all is sound which others leave,
You come not crediting half your bailiff says.

He told you all, an honest labourer.
But had not noticed this, that in the year
When you were born a twist of feckless wind
Brought one small seed and left it on the ground
Between the chance and choice to live or die.
It drew the means of living undeterred,
    Uncurling in the shell it stirred,
To rise, and sway upon your property.

Its art is merely holding to the earth —
But see how confidently, from its birth,
Its branches, lifting above failures, keep
Vigour within the discipline of shape.
Come here, friend, yearly, till you've carved the bark
With all the old virtues, young in fibre, names
    That swell with time and tree ; no dreams,
No ornaments, but tallies for your work.

Kingsley Amis

MASTERS

THAT horse whose rider fears to jump will fall,
Riflemen miss if orders sound unsure ;
They only are secure who seem secure ;
    Who lose their voice, lose all.

Those whom heredity or guns have made
Masters, must show it by a common speech ;
Expected words in the same tone from each
    Will always be obeyed.

Likewise with stance, with gestures, and with face ;
No more than mouth need move when words are said,
No more than hand to strike, or point ahead ;
    Like slaves, limbs learn their place.

In triumph as in mutiny unmoved,
These make their public act their private good,
Their words in lounge or courtroom understood,
    But themselves never loved.

The eyes that will not look, the twitching cheek,
The hands that sketch what mouth would fear to own,
These only make us known, and we are known
    Only as we are weak :

By yielding mastery the will is freed,
For it is by surrender that we live,
And we are taken if we wish to give,
    Are needed if we need.

WRONG WORDS

HALF shut, our eye dawdles down the page
Seeing the word love, the word death, the word life,
Rhyme-words of poets in a silver age :
Silver of the bauble, not of the knife.

Too fluent, drenching with confectionery
One image, one event's hard outline,
The words of failure's voluptuary
Descant around love — love of a routine.

There follow high words from a thwarted child
Rightly denied what it would foul, threatening
Grown-ups with its death, eager to gild
The pose of writhing with the pose of resigning.

But loneliness, the word never said,
Pleads to be recognised through their conceits ;
Behind their frantic distortion lies the dread,
Unforced, unblurred, of real defeats :

Their real ladies would not follow the book,
Wrong ladies, happy with wrong words, wrong lives ;
Careening now, they blazed, while none would look,
The distress signals of their superlatives.

AGAINST ROMANTICISM

A TRAVELLER who walks a temperate zone
  — Woods devoid of beasts, roads that please the foot —
Finds that its decent surface grows too thin :
  Something unperceived fumbles at his nerves.
To please an ingrown taste for anarchy
  Torrid images circle in the wood,
And sweat for recognition up the road,
  Cramming close the air with their bookish cries.
All senses then are glad to gasp : the eye
  Smeared with garish paints, tickled up with ghosts
That brandish warnings or an abstract noun ;
  Melodies from shards, memories from coal,
Or saws from powdered tombstones thump the ear ;
  Bodies rich with heat wriggle to the touch,
And verbal scents made real spellbind the nose :
  Incense, frankincense ; legendary the taste
Of drinks or fruits or tongues laid on the tongue.
  Over all, a grand meaning fills the scene,
And sets the brain raging with prophecy,
  Raging to discard real time and place,
Raging to build a better time and place
  Than the ones which give prophecy its field
To work, the calm material for its rage,
  And the context which makes it prophecy.

Better, of course, if images were plain,
  Warnings clearly said, shapes put down quite still
Within the fingers' reach, or else nowhere ;
  But complexities crowd the simplest thing,
And flaw the surface that they cannot break.
  Let us make at least visions that we need :
Let mine be pallid, so that it cannot
  Force a single glance, form a single word ;

An afternoon long-drawn and silent, with
   Buildings free from all grime of history,
The people total strangers, the grass cut,
   Not long, voluble swooning wilderness,
And green, not parched or soured by frantic suns
   Doubling the commands of a rout of gods,
Nor trampled by the havering unicorn ;
   Let the sky be clean of officious birds
Punctiliously flying on the left ;
   Let there be a path leading out of sight,
And at its other end a temperate zone :
   Woods devoid of beasts, roads that please the foot.

SOMETHING NASTY IN THE BOOKSHOP

BETWEEN the GARDENING and the COOKERY
   Comes the brief POETRY shelf ;
By the Nonesuch Donne, a thin anthology
   Offers itself.

Critical, and with nothing else to do,
   I scan the Contents page,
Relieved to find the names are mostly new ;
   No one my age.

Like all strangers, they divide by sex :
   Landscape near Parma
Interests a man, so does *The Double Vortex*,
   So does *Rilke and Buddha*.

'I travel, you see', 'I think' and 'I can read'
   These titles seem to say ;
But *I Remember You, Love is my Creed,*
   Poem for J.,

The ladies' choice, discountenance my patter
    For several seconds ;
From somewhere in this (as in any) matter
    A moral beckons.

Should poets bicycle-pump the human heart
    Or squash it flat ?
Man's love is of man's life a thing apart ;
    Girls aren't like that.

We men have got love well weighed up ; our stuff
    Can get by without it.
Women don't seem to think that's good enough ;
    They write about it,

And the awful way their poems lay them open
    Just doesn't strike them.
Women are really much nicer than men :
    No wonder we like them.

Deciding this, we can forget those times
    We sat up half the night
Chock-full of love, crammed with bright thoughts,
        names, rhymes,
    And couldn't write.

HERE IS WHERE

HERE, *where the ragged water*
Is twilled and spun over
Pebbles backed like beetles,
Bright as beer-bottles,

Bits of it like snow beaten
Or milk boiling in saucepan . . .

Going well so far, eh ?
But soon, I'm sorry to say,
The here-where recipe
Will have to intrude its *I*,
Its main verb *want*,
Its *this* at some tangent.

What has this subject
Got to do with that object ?
Why drag in
All that water and stone ?
Scream the place down *here*,
There's nobody *there*.

The country, to townies,
Is hardly more than nice,
A window-box, pretty
When the afternoon's empty ;
When a visitor waits,
The window shuts.

NOCTURNE

UNDER the winter street-lamps, near the bus-stop,
Two people with nowhere to go fondle each other,
Writhe slowly in the entrance to a shop.
In the intervals of watching them, a sailor
Yaws about with an empty beer-flagon,
Looking for something good to smash it on.

48

Mere animals : on this the Watch Committee
And myself seem likely to agree ;
But all this fumbling about, this wasteful
Voiding of sweat and breath — is that *animal* ?

Nothing so sure and economical.

These keep the image of another creature
In crippled versions, cocky, drab and stewed ;
What beast holds off its paw to gesture,
Or gropes towards being understood ?

THE VOICE OF AUTHORITY
A Language Game

Do this. Don't move. O'Grady says do this,
You get a move on, see, do what I say.
Look lively when I say O'Grady says.

Say this. Shut up. O'Grady says say this,
You talk fast without thinking what to say.
What goes is what I say O'Grady says.

Or let me rather put the point like this :
O'Grady says what goes is what I say
O'Grady says ; that's what O'Grady says.

By substituting you can shorten this,
Since any god you like will do to say
The things you like, that's what O'Grady says.

The harm lies not in that, but in that this
Progression's first and last terms are I say
O'Grady says, not just O'Grady says.

Yet it's O'Grady must be out of this
Before what we say goes, not what we say
O'Grady says. Or so O'Grady says.

DEPARTURE

FOR one month afterwards the eye stays true,
And sees the other's face held still and free
Of ornament ; then tires of peering down
A narrow vista, and the month runs out.

Too lax, this eye will crave the merit of
A faithful sentry frozen at his post,
And not a movement seen ; yet ranges over
Far other tracts, its object lost, corrupt.

Nor should I now swell to halloo the names
Of feelings that no one needs to remember,
Nor caper with my spray of wilted avowals
To clutter up your path I should wish clear.

Perhaps it is not too late to crane the eye
And find you, distant and small, but as you are ;
If not, I will retain you honestly blurred,
Not a bland refraction of sweet mirrors.

THE SOURCES OF THE PAST

A BROKEN flower-stem, a broken vase,
    A match-box torn in two and thrown

Among the lumps of glass :
    At the last meeting, these alone
Record its ruptures, point its violence,
    And, it seems, are ready to maintain
This charted look of permanence
    In the first moment's pain.

But now the door slams, the steps retreat ;
    Into one softness night will blur
The diverse, the hard street ;
    And memory will soon prefer
That polished set of symbols, glass and rose
    (By slight revision), to the real mess
Of stumbling, arguing, yells, blows
    Or tears : to real distress.

All fragments of the past, near and far,
    Come down to us framed in a calm
No contemplations jar ;
    But they grub it up from lapse of time,
And, could we strip that firm order away,
    What crude agitation would be shown :
What aimless hauntings behind clay,
    What fevers behind stone ?

D. J. Enright

WAITING FOR THE BUS

SHE hung away her years, her eyes grew young,
  And filled the dress that filled the shop ;
Her figure softened into summer, though wind stung
  And rain would never stop.

A dreaming not worn out with knowing,
A moment's absence from the watch, the weather.
  I threw the paper down, that carried no such story,
But roared for what it could not have, perpetual health
    and liberty and glory.
  It whirled away, a lost bedraggled feather.

Then have we missed the bus ? Or are we sure
    which way the wind is blowing ?

EVENING IN THE KHAMSIN

SLOWLY the sea grows pale, and the sun grows more
    precise,
Shrinking into its slimmer contours, its fear makes us afraid.
The gold in the dying sky dies slowly to silver — but what,
More horribly, is happening in the flattened sea ?

Like a frightened cat it crouches, sleek and slightly arched,
The changing lights betray the churning hidden bowels,
A slow sick swell, the tension in the falling line of foam.
What of us, when our blue and boastful sea lies so
    unnerved ?

The silver sun is yellow, now the yellow sun is green : the sky
No longer alight, now the sky is heavy and near.   The thick
    air sighs,
And the light around us slowly moulders — but what,
More dreadful, mercifully distant, happens beneath the
    sea's tight skin ?

Not now the enamelled lido, with its brown and holiday
    bodies,
The confident beach, with the clipped claws of the breaking
    wave.
But a thick green swirl, it seems, of rotted bodies, putrescent
    cream —
All the dead of the great seas, gathered together here, still
    inarticulate ?

And then in the falling darkness the flying sand is annulled,
Only our cheeks still sting a little, a little grit between the
    teeth :
The street lamps all burst out, dim yet stronger than that
    great defeated sun,
And across the mollified waters the pathways of gold grow
    firm.

BAIE DES ANGES, NICE

W AS Freud entirely right ?   We rise to chase those inner
    phantoms,

54

Who often end by chasing us.   The sleeping dogs
Start up from every corner : they have not read the text-
     books
That bid us pat their heads.   The only bone they want
     is us.

    .   .   .   .   .

The villas turn and twist, like orchids, multi-coloured on
     the terraced hills.
Amazed, the palm-tree flaunts its plumper head, its feet in
     fertile soil ;
The olives billow up like smoke, piebald among the darker
     leaves,
While orange crowds out lemon, the vine creeps when and
     where it may,
And roses grow like grass.

And yet the blue sky wanes, the blue sea turns to lead :
The painted villas blanch and shrink, as massive, metallic,
The clouds climb down the mountains, and dry lightning
     spurts among the trees.

Nothing by halves.   This richness is a passion that never
     rests,
From ripeness moves to raging, from the knotted rosebud
     to the scattered leaves.
Proud mountain, luminous citron, azure coast — they do
     not grow
Without the shrivelling thunderbolt, the tired and flaking
     walls.

The storm passes and the bay once more is full of angels.
The sea's harp ripples and the air is sharp with sudden
     scents :

55

Cafés and cars disgorge — good, bad, indifferent — and the
  bay is full of men.

                    .   .   .   .   .

Was Goethe wholly wrong ? It is by onward striding
We lay our ghosts, he said. Seeking neither to avoid nor
  meet.
No tree stays small through fear of meeting lightning :
The strawberry finds its ripeness in the straw. They grow,
  or rest,
In light or darkness. Doing what they have to do,
And suffering what, and only what, they must.

THE LAUGHING HYENA, BY HOKUSAI

FOR him, it seems, everything was molten. Court-ladies
  flow in gentle streams,
Or, gathering lotus, strain sideways from their curving boat,
A donkey prances, or a kite dances in the sky, or soars like
  sacrificial smoke.
All is flux : waters fall and leap, and bridges leap and fall.
Even his Tortoise undulates, and his Spring Hat is lively as
  a pool of fish.
All he ever saw was sea : a sea of marble splinters —
Long bright fingers claw across his pages, fjords and islands
  and shattered trees —

And the Laughing Hyena, cavalier of evil, as volcanic as the
  rest :
Elegant in a flowered gown, a face like a bomb-burst,
Featured with fangs and built about a rigid laugh,
Ever moving, like a pond's surface where a corpse has sunk.

Between the raised talons of the right hand rests an object —
At rest, like a pale island in a savage sea — a child's head,
Immobile, authentic, torn and bloody —
The point of repose in the picture, the point of movement
    in us.

Terrible enough, this demon.   Yet it is present and perfect,
Firm as its horns, curling among its thick and handsome
    hair.
I find it an honest visitant, even consoling, after all
Those sententious phantoms, choked with rage and un-
    certainty,
Who grimace from contemporary pages.   It, at least,
Knows exactly why it laughs.

ON THE DEATH OF A CHILD

THE greatest griefs shall find themselves inside the
    smallest cage.
It's only then that we can hope to tame their rage.

The monsters we must live with.   For it will not do
To hiss humanity because one human threw
Us out of heart and home.   Or part

At odds with life because one baby failed to live.
Indeed, as little as its subject, is the wreath we give —

The big words fail to fit.   Like giant boxes
Round small bodies.   Taking up improper room,
Where so much withering is, and so much bloom.

57

MID-MEDITERRANEAN: SEPTEMBER
EVENING

IT is like a smart display of patterns in excellent taste,
And most remarkable is the sense of differing fabrics —
As the sun declines, as clouds affect its shapes and colours,
The sea, the scene, is changed — from tapestry to oilcloth,
Oilcloth to glazed ceramic, to coarse strong carpet work,
And watered silk, stained glass, and back to tapestry.

It is not the commercial blue we are concerned with, or the
     trite designs of foam,
But colours which are textures, textures which are shapes,
And always changing — not with kaleidoscopic jerk like
     soldiers changing guard,
But always a pattern and scheme, and never an empty
     moment while the scene is dressed.

The elongated rainbow eyes, the oily wells, the diamond
     lozenges of purple, brown and blue,
The jellying flanks of blue and black that burst and fuse
     like mercury,
And run along the ship.   And now a perfect net of narrow
     squares
That catches the sea tightly, like sleeping leviathan.

And this is the eastern sea.   While on the western plains
The waters are coagulate with huge and vivid colours —
The pattern's lost : with shameless rhetoric the old sun
     makes his exit :
Thunder shakes the gallery : and they are deaf and blind.

NIGHTLONG they chatter and declaim, the frogs,
And much of what they say is lies, perhaps,
And love and lies. And yet all rises
Into the ripened air and is forgiven.
            The fireflies glance aside,
Those painted insects, in their nervous dance :
Grace in the body burns, although the soul has
        charred, perhaps,

And hard and huge, stars shift in silence, coins in his
        crowded purse —
Night swaggers, sings or sobs, unplanned,
Among quick crickets and voluptuous vines : no
        calculation guides
His warm and soft and moist and generous hand.

What do they say of us, in our firm distant island ?
They'll not forgive us soon : for we were always right,
And always said so : we reached conclusion quickly,
Along sad Roman roads : beer and long-suffering,
Both were our brewing, both made us slightly dull.
            Our coldness quenched the fireflies,
We choked the frogs off with a formal note.

LOST, STOLEN OR STRAYED

UNDER the moon the frosty glint of the pale tar patches,
The sudden gallabiehs billowing up like jinn, all night
The one long cigarette despairingly sucked — and all
That memory hesitates to declare : cheap bitter wine
Grazing the throat, and cheap thoughts too muddled to be
        bitter.

The polyglot patron with caressing hand and careful hair,
The drunken secret policeman too drunk to be true,
The servile dubious company so eager to be of use,
The last sour jerk of energy that slaps back the rising stairs.

And even so the safe arrival against remarkable odds —
Smarter at arithmetic than waiters, innocent among thieves,
Proficient in native cursing against the naked boys,
The menacing bats fobbed off with magnificent gestures,
God's hand against the traffic, an acrobat's foot on the
    tram —

Not utterly lost, these week-ends, but soared through like a
    bird
Astray and rather silly.   Is home at the end ?
Wait, not too wild, and see.

THE INTERPRETERS
(or, How to Bury Yourself in a Book)

WHY have they stripped the grass from the sides of the
    road,
leaving the worms agape, and a senseless load
of brick-ends and broken glass ?   Tomorrow it will
start to show again.   For that is what it means.

One thinks of those critics for whom the outside is a dread-
    ful bore :
they scrape for the ambiguous, dig for the profound, deep,
    deep beneath the ground —
what you read on the surface of the agitated page is only an
    idle dusty weed.

The poet mentions suffering and even starvation ;
dead cats in the street and women slowly dying on the
     streets ;
the lot of a sizable part of a sizable nation —
but dear me no ! — that will not do for the critic, that
     connoisseur of words
who cannot abide the crude vulgarity of meaning —
his expertise, my dear, merits something richer
than these ancient histories of anguish and horror or an
     empty belly's tasteless keening.

They have sliced the grass away, they are poking
their ingenious lancets in the damp inhuman earth —
around them the blown rice limps to its harvest, a child
     runs to its ambiguous birth,
the peasants look at their rotting cabbages,
a gang of clods are building a block of flats.

But the scholars are chasing a glittering fragment
of Zen or the cracked semblance of an Emblem —
for it is not what a poem merely says that matters,
elsewhere than here it finds its true signification :
     whore, you may be sure,
refers to some mysterious metaphysical temptation ;
hunger was his image for a broken dream ; bread
an old religious symbol ; his typhoons the wind of God.

Good lord, if a poet really meant what he said,
we should all be out of a job — why on earth
would he sing of the merely real ? — the papers have taken
     up that chorus —
'the agonies, the strife of human hearts' ? — why, Hollywood
     will do that for us.

61

The peasants have salvaged their cabbages ; the block
of flats is nearly as ready as its tenants ; somewhere
someone saves a child from a swollen river,
and really means it —
        the critics in their studies, collate as ever
their absences of meanings, unvexing and unvexed —
        but the grass waves high on the road again,
and the roots refer to the text.

THE WONDERING SCHOLAR

HE went a little queer. He could not really think the land
        was wholly waste,
The peasants all unholy. More and more the rice-plants
        twinkled in their muddy glory.
He failed to ask that every summer should be full of
        swallows.

He ran away, then walked, from those stern masters of the
        sleepy hollows,
And found, beyond the weeping willows, a world quite
        large and rich in men as good and bad as he.
His standards slipped and fell. Not every alley hid a
        thief, not every thief stripped all.
The lines which creased men's faces, he discovered
That some were caused by grief, and some by laughter.
He ceased to stalk the dusty city, like some lustful critic,
        after
A nasty traffic accident, or bent on finding tawdry rhythms
        and false rhyme.
He sought to broaden his acquaintanceship with style.

The only time that he was ridden by
Sat on his wrist or in his diary.   That he obeyed — the rest
    was his to ride.
Does the silk-worm know the looms of Nishijin ? — '*I* shall
    not tell them,' he replied.
A giggling cry behind the paper screen did not portend the
    bad end of a race
Or mean the death of every god.   Better to do what little
Could be done — a tip, he came to feel, and not a tract.
       He visited that lovely cataract
Where the desperate look and leap.   He looked.
Back in the whirling city, he watched the chopsticks curling
    on the oily river,
And recalled that he should feel defiled, that he should
    weep.
       That talent, too, had gone.   He smiled.

He came to see how even those who could not read had
    pleasures —
Cynic, he asked himself, or simpleton ?   He strolled
    between inexplicable banners, under a sky
Rolled round by foreign tongues, and found that he was
    reading less and less.
It was the emotions of people that surprised him vastly,
    not of poets —
Those were his task at school, these were a job for life.
His poems grew shorter and shorter.   Yet he had seen the
    lion lie down with the lamb.
He died reluctantly, but happy — 'Down to earth is what
    I am.'

Donald Davie

THE FOUNTAIN

FEATHERS up fast, steeples, and then in clods
Thuds into its first basin ; thence as surf
Smokes up and hangs ; irregularly slops
Into its second, tattered like a shawl ;
There, chill as rain, stipples a danker green,
Where urgent tritons lob their heavy jets.

For Berkeley this was human thought, that mounts
From bland assumptions to inquiring skies,
There glints with wit, fumes into fancies, plays
With its negations, and at last descends
As by a law of nature to its bowl
Of thus enlightened but still common sense.

We who have no such confidence must gaze
With all the more affection on these forms,
These spires, these plumes, these calm reflections, these
Similitudes of surf and turf and shawl,
Graceful returns upon acceptances.
We ask of fountains only that they play,

Though that was not what Berkeley meant at all.

A HEAD PAINTED BY DANIEL O'NEILL

DIASTASIS, the space between the eyes,
And not that either, but the two eyes' two beams,
Those, and the space between them,
Here pierce our wall ; which yet remains as blank
As if this window were for looking in
And never out, or if for looking out,
Then out upon a meadow that, unpeopled,
Was yet so far from ever being empty
One could not say it was a view commanded
By us or by our window, since indeed
The view itself commanded us, and watched.

Of those we know we say that one or two
Have a commanding presence, but of none,
He is that presence, is himself, as you,
Beautiful head in session, president,
Are just yourself and beautiful.   And yet
Perfection looking out at imperfection
Must find the human spectacle forbidding
As any field of presences, or rather
As any field of action ; since for her
We have reserved the painfully condensed,
Inactive rôle of being beautiful.

Yes, presences at home with presences
Can only brood and move us to repose ;
Our broken-ness can burn across the air.
Outsiders looking in at her affairs
In such good order, sealed and settled so,
When you encounter her composure there,
Old as the sill she sits on, gazing out
Upon the scene of all our darting loves,
Our looks that kill and move momentously,

Think she's as puzzled as inscrutable.
Be stilled, not daunted, by her steadiness.

REJOINDER TO A CRITIC

You may be right : 'How can I dare to feel ?'
May be the only question I can pose,
'And haply by abstruse research to steal
From my own nature all the natural man'
My sole resource. And I do not suppose
That others may not have a better plan.

And yet I'll quote again, and gloss it too
(You know by now my liking for *collage*) :
Donne could be daring, but he never knew,
When he inquired, 'Who's injured by my love ?'
Love's radio-active fall-out on a large
Expanse around the point it bursts above.

'Alas, alas, who's injured by my love ?'
And recent history answers : Half Japan !
Not love, but hate ? Well, both are versions of
The 'feeling' that you dare me to. Be dumb !
Appear concerned only to make it scan !
How dare we now be anything but numb ?

CHERRY RIPE
On a Painting by Juan Gris

No ripening curve can be allowed to sag
On cubist's canvas or in sculptor's stone :

Informal fruit, that burgeons from the swag,
Would spoil the ripening that is art's alone.

This can be done with cherries. Other fruit
Have too much bloom of import, like the grape,
Whose opulence comes welling from a root
Struck far too deep to yield so pure a shape.

And Cherry ripe, indeed ripe, ripe, I cry.
Let orchards flourish in the poet's soul
And bear their feelings that are mastered by
Maturing rhythms, to compose a whole.

But how the shameful grapes and olives swell,
Excrescent from no cornucopia, tart,
Too near to oozing to be handled well :
Ripe, ripe, they cry, and perish in my heart.

TOO LATE FOR SATIRE

WHOM I have knives for could begin with you,
The less than pedant, being charlatan
In even that pretension ; or with you,
Whose second nature is the sycophant,
For whom to fawn is not to play a role
(Elaborately humorous and bland),
But the unguarded habit of the soul.

Stiff in your drapes with a heraldic air
Your bosom follies bleed upon the brand ;
And yet ensues no cleansing of the air.
These exorcisms are the irrelevant
Vocabulary of another age

(The sycophant, the pedant, and the pimp,
Like quaint engravings on a deckled page.)

I might have been as pitiless as Pope
But to no purpose ; in a tragic age
We share the hatred but we lack the hope
By pinning follies to reform the age.
To blame is lame, and satirists are late.
No knife can stick in history or the id,
No cutlass carve us from the lime of fate.

LIMITED ACHIEVEMENT
(Piranesi, *Prisons*, Plate VI)

SEEING his stale vocabulary build
The same décor — observe this 'gloomy vault' —
We tire of this good fellow, highly skilled
No doubt, but pertinacious to a fault.

The same few dismal properties, the same
Oppressive air of justified unease,
Proclaim the practised hand from which they came,
Although these show a willingness to please.

Yes, some attempt undoubtedly was made
To lift the composition, and to pierce
The bald tympana — vainly, I'm afraid ;
The effect remains, as ever, gaunt and fierce.

Those were his true proclivities ? Perhaps.
Successful in his single narrow track,
He branches out, but only to collapse,
Imprisoned in his own unhappy knack,

Which, when unfailing, fails him most, perhaps.

One simple and effective rhyme
Over and over in the April light ;
   And a touch of the old time
In the serving-man, stooping, aproned tight,
At the end of the dappled avenue
To the easy phrase, 'tereu-tereu',
Mulled over by the sleepy dove —
This was the poem I had to write.

White wall where the creepers climb
Year after year on the sunny side ;
   And a touch of the old time
In the sandalled Capuchin's silent stride
Over the shadows and through the clear
Cushion-soft wooing of the ear
From two meadows away, by the dove —
This was the poem that was denied.

For whether it was the friar's crime,
His leanness suddenly out of tune ;
   — Or a touch of the old time
In the given phrase, with its unsought boon
Of a lax autumnal atmosphere,
Seemed quaint and out of keeping here,
I do not know.   I know the dove
Outsang me down the afternoon.

REMEMBERING THE 'THIRTIES

I

HEARING one saga, we enact the next.
We please our elders when we sit enthralled ;

But then they're puzzled ; and at last they're vexed
To have their youth so avidly recalled.

It dawns upon the veterans after all
That what for them were agonies, to us
Are high-brow thrillers, though historical ;
And all their feats quite strictly fabulous.

This novel written fifteen years ago,
Set in my boyhood and my boyhood home,
These poems about 'abandoned workings', show
Worlds more remote than Ithaca or Rome.

The Anschluss, Guernica — all the names
At which those poets thrilled, or were afraid,
For me mean schools and schoolmasters and games ;
And in the process someone is betrayed.

Ourselves perhaps.   The Devil for a joke
Might carve his own initials on our desk,
And still we'd miss the point, because he spoke
An idiom too dated, Audenesque.

Ralegh's Guiana also killed his son.
A pretty pickle if we came to see
The tallest story really packed a gun,
The Telemachiad an Odyssey.

II

Even to them the tales were not so true
As not to be ridiculous as well :
The ironmaster met his Waterloo,
But Rider Haggard rode along the fell.

'Leave for Cape Wrath to-night!' They lounged away
On Fleming's trek or Isherwood's ascent.
England expected every man that day
To show his motives were ambivalent.

They played the fool, not to appear as fools
In time's long glass. A deprecating air
Disarmed, they thought, the jeers of later schools :
Yet irony itself is doctrinaire,

And, curiously, nothing now betrays
Their type to time's derision like this coy
Insistence on the quizzical, their craze
For showing Hector was a mother's boy.

A neutral tone is nowadays preferred.
And yet it may be better, if we must,
To find the stance impressive and absurd
Than not to see the hero for the dust.

For courage is the vegetable king,
The sprig of all ontologies, the weed
That beards the slag-heap with its hectoring,
Whose green adventure is to run to seed.

Robert Conquest

EPISTEMOLOGY OF POETRY

ACROSS the long-curved bight or bay
The waves move clear beneath the day
And rolling in obliquely each
Unwinds its white torque up the beach.

Beneath the full semantic sun
The twisting currents race and run.
Words and evaluations start.
And yet the verse should play its part.

Below a certain threshold light
Is insufficient to excite
Those mechanisms which the eye
Constructs its daytime objects by :

A different system wakes behind
The dark, wide pupils till the mind
Accepts an image of this sea
As clear, but in an altered key.

Now darkness falls.   And poems attempt
Light reconciling done and dreamt.

73

I do not find it in the rash
Disruption of the lightning flash.

Those vivid rigours stun the verse
And neural structure still prefers
The moon beneath whose moderate light
The great seas glitter in the bight.

NANTUCKET

It lay in the mist or the wind.

Perhaps Karlsefni saw it to starboard
On the voyage to Hóp from Straumfjord.

Fishermen, farmers and theologians
Settled the swept bay and the crescent bluffs.

And then its attention was filled with whales.
A blunt, chipped sickle : it reaped the sea.
Oh that was an astonishing empire !
All the oceans gave up to its hunters
Dangerous and profitable monsters.
Folgers and Husseys, Starbucks and Coffins,
Branded the salt wrath with their keels and spears.

Melville chose them, the boldest men on earth,
To be his champions on the demon seas
Of his heart. Even they succumbed.
Ahab died. The waters washed
The ruined survivor to another coast.

The whaling went elsewhere, to techniques and guns.
And the island lies in its parish, weather and past.

ANTHÉOR

A HEAVY light hangs in these silent airs.
Out to the west the failing day prepares
A sultry splendour. Lying on the cliff
I watch the little bay below, the beach,
Red rocks, the slow vibrations of the sea,
Gazing deep into it all as if
  I could find beneath it the truth
  And be free.

What can a poem do with a landscape? What
Extract that pure philosophies cannot?
Express the universe in terms of parts
Chosen to illustrate all time and space,
Deducing then beyond those images
The general essence of all human hearts
  And the most transitory look
  On a face?

The emblems are too crude. The poetry sees
A giant static set-piece where the trees'
Variety shows a single streak of green,
Or overcharged intense cosmographies
Where the light becomes too fluid, spills and soaks
Washing away the landscape's flickering screen,
  And the hot stars crackle
  In a sky of ice.

Even the parts escape the dying words.
How can they seize precisely on that bird's
White spiral past the bastion of red rock?
Even the redness is too subtle for
The inexact impressions of a phrase

That draws strength only from the hard-won stock
   Of image flowering from
   Our speech's core.

But word and image, the whole outer song
Can only live as surface to the strong
Thrust of the poet's whole self and language into
Perfection of his knowledge and his life,
Which unintentioned still selects the detail
From sense and vision which may help it win to
   Its own interpretation of
   That hieroglyph.

And yet each day provides its contribution
Of vision to constructing that solution.
And working, upon these red cliffs today,
To let the static and the moving reach
Their place inside one complex of relations,
I find a tentative image in the bay :
   It is the waves of the sea
   On its beach.

IN THE RHODOPE

THE poem tries to speak of the heart
And to relate it to the natural plectrum
Which plucks so clear a note out of its sunlight,
To make its vague, neglected virtues flare
From the ocean and air.

But how does the poem come ?
Its voices bubbling from a pool of darkness

To a deliberate fruit of grapes and peaches ?
Or striking a horror and a melody at night
Down corridors of dead light ?

And how does it distort ?
Like the pearl-diver's hand trembling under water
Towards his stone of food and beauty ?   Or
Absolute mirage into a lonely eye
Out of the swan sky ?

— Let me write one more poem,
About this lake at night, black with a golden ice,
Or some green transparent atmosphere at daybreak
Made beautiful by that strange illumination
That poets are always working to bring out
— The colour of doubt.

DÉDÉE D'ANVERS

AROUND the iron bed the camera moves
Or follows where, across the fog-wet stone
She and her life, like one automaton,
Run to exhaustion down the usual grooves.

Quick with desire to glimpse the unobsessed
It switches restlessly from view to view,
Pauses an instant on a seeming clue ;
Rejects it ; and resumes its nervous quest.

Till in that trajectory of fear and boredom
Letting the iron twilight slip and slough
Life burns through briefly to its inch of freedom,

And in the flicker of a lens or eye
Forms to one microcosm of all love
A woman's body and her fantasy.

THE ROKEBY VENUS

LIFE pours out images, the accidental
At once deleted when the purging mind
Detects their resonance as inessential :
Yet these may leave some fruitful trace behind.

Thus on this painted mirror is projected
The shield that rendered safe the Gorgon's head.
A travesty. — Yet even as reflected
The young face seems to strike us, if not dead,

At least into an instantaneous winter
Which life and reason can do nothing with,
Freezing the watcher and the painting into
A single immobility of myth.

But underneath the pigments' changeless weather
The artist only wanted to devise
A posture that could show him, all together,
Face, shoulders, waist, delectable smooth thighs.

So with the faulty image as a start
We come at length to analyse and name
The luminous darkness in the depths of art :
The timelessness that holds us is the same

As that of the transcendent sexual glance,
And art grows brilliant in the light it sheds,

Direct or not, on the inhabitants
Of our imaginations and our beds.

HUMANITIES

HYPNOTIZED and told they're seeing red
When really looking at a yellow wall
The children speak of orange seen instead :
Split to such rainbow through that verbal lens
It takes a whole heart's effort to see all
The human plenum as a single ens.

The word on the objective breath must be
A wind to winnow the emotive out ;
Music can generalize the inner sea
In dark harmonics of a blinded heart ;
But, hot with certainty and keen with doubt,
Verse sweats out heartfelt knowledge, clear-eyed
    art.

Is it, when paper roses make us sneeze,
A mental or a physical event ?
The word can freeze us to such categories,
Yet verse can warm the mirrors of the word
And through their loose distortions represent
The scene, the heart, the life, as they occurred.

— In a dream's blueness or a sunset's bronze
Poets seek the images of love and wonder,
But absolutes of music, gold or swans
Are only froth unless they go to swell

That harmony of science pealing under
The poem's waters like a sunken bell.

NEAR JAKOBSELV

DWARF willow, bilberry, bogcotton ; a land of lakes,
And to the north a flat transparent ocean
That stretches to the ice-cap.   For those millions
Of frozen tons are always somewhere there,
Though out of sight now and far at the back of the mind
In the long hot day and the green efflorescence.

The insects pipe and drone.   The arctic sky,
A very pale blue, completely bare of cloud,
Lays down its haunting midnight on the tundra.
There is no human trace for hours behind us,
And now we lie and sleep, or watch the new

Arctic world that rises like a mayfly
Out of each melting winter and never grows old,
But dies.   Nothing here
Is in connexion with the central planet,
With the long histories and the human vision.

Its images are not ours.   This speed and brightness
Are innocent of purpose.   And in that huge returning
Winter that waits in the north there is no moral
— The ice bears no relation to the anger.
I lie and listen

To the desolating cry of an eagle.
                                        Perhaps

This very newness and this isolation
May strike some hidden tremor in the heart
And make its rock gush water.
                              My companion
Sleeps, scarcely breathing, on the blue-green lichen.
And a faint unchanging radiance plays on us
Out of the whole young landscape, as I lie and watch or
    hours
The motionless lake and the grebe diving.

John Wain

REASON FOR NOT WRITING
ORTHODOX NATURE POETRY

THE January sky is deep and calm.
The mountain sprawls in comfort, and the sea
Sleeps in the crook of that enormous arm.

And Nature from a simple recipe —
Rocks, water, mist, a sunlit winter's day —
Has brewed a cup whose strength has dizzied me.

So little beauty is enough to pay ;
The heart so soon yields up its store of love,
And where you love you cannot break away.

So sages never found it hard to prove
Nor prophets to declare in metaphor
That God and Nature must be hand in glove,

And this became the basis of their lore.
Then later poets found it easy going
To give the public what they bargained for,

And like a spectacled curator showing
The wares of his museum to the crowd,
They yearly waxed more eloquent and knowing

More slick, more photographic, and more proud :
From Tennyson with notebook in his hand
(His truth to Nature fits him like a shroud)

To moderns who devoutly hymn the land.
So be it : each is welcome to his voice ;
They are a gentle, if a useless, band.

But leave me free to make a sterner choice ;
Content, without embellishment, to note
How little beauty bids the heart rejoice,

How little beauty catches at the throat.
Simply, I love this mountain and this bay
With love that I can never speak by rote,

And where you love you cannot break away.

MINUTES OF THE LAST MEETING

' tomorrow is our permanent address '
E. E. CUMMINGS.

As an address it pleased us for a while.
We liked to mention it before our friends ;
Printed on notepaper, it gave us style.

We issued invitations at week-ends ;
Even relations thought they ought to call,
Forgave our failures ; we had made amends.

Only the calendar upon the wall
Uttered a warning note : 'This is tomorrow' ;
Hinted that climbers had been known to fall.

To pay our debts, of course, we had to borrow,
But still the poet taught us what to say :
'The roots are cut that bound us to our sorrow.'

We hated most the calm official way
The postman knocked each morning with a sheaf
Of letters forwarded from yesterday.

We opened them, curt notes of disbelief,
Skimmed through them, laughed, and tore them into
    spills ;
But this, unhappily, brought no relief,

Because the bloody things were always bills.

WHO SPEAKS MY LANGUAGE?
(I)

Who that has ever tried to speak his mind,
Assuming that his mind holds more than blended
Refuse that other minds have dropped behind,

Can feel assured his words were comprehended ?
Did those who listened get the message right,
Could they repeat the tale when it was ended ?

Ah, no. It seems the simplest words take fright
And shape themselves anew for every ear,
Protected by a crazy copyright

From ever making their intention clear.
And yet one cannot blame the words alone ;
Why do they obstinately disappear

Back into the top hat whence they are shown
Because the conjurer himself is slack ?
Because his patter stales, his act outgrown ?

For see : the audience has turned its back.

WHO SPEAKS MY LANGUAGE?
(III)

Now another reason for sad misgiving
applying even to those who are living
by my calendar and in my region
and with many other signs of cohesion
is one not often treated in poetry
(and therefore I adopt this fluency
of drabness in stumbling anyday speech)
in a word, MONEY. I could reach
many who would find my words familiar
were their and my incomes more similar :
but those who have money cannot imagine
what could possibly be the fashion
of life for those whose daily struggle
is increased to just about double
by lack of short cuts : while the rest,
those whose share is no more than crust,
are altogether too deeply
caught in the mesh of the weekly
drudge and traipse of existence
in a world of delay and distance
even to hear if I shouted,
even to ask What about it.

And so the pounds, shillings and pence
have built up a sound-proof fence.
For who can follow my drift
if he need toil at no craft?
Yet, once dragged out from behind
his bank balance and bound
to earn his bread by a trade,
be it at ledger or lathe,
he sinks to a level of drabness
beyond reach of my joy or my sadness.

Alas, the millions whom currency
has made deaf to my urgency!

WHO SPEAKS MY LANGUAGE?
(IV)

AND then there is the question of how far
You can expect the Common Man to share
Your own concern with words and what they are.

The shades of meaning hover in the air,
But when you want to point to one precisely
The others cannot see them glowing there.

You dare not speak too primly or concisely
Because your hearers for their simple needs
Feel that a few crass gestures will do nicely,

Words being just a feeble kind of deeds.
It puzzles them that you should spend your time
Coaxing the wind to touch strategic reeds;

And like the rope trick boy, they think, you
    climb
Up nothing, and achieve a senseless poise ;
Reasoning thus : a poem is a rhyme,

And language quite a useful kind of noise.

USEFULNESS OF LIGHT

STIRRED by the wind's long spoon
the snow for one whole day
spins down. The sky comes clean.
Colour is here to stay.

Night circles past. Again
light stirs. The sun bangs down.
Again the world comes clean.
The sun speaks to the town.

The sun bangs down its rays
like coins to buy the earth.
The wind's long spoon is poised.
Something is brought to birth.

Love is the something, since
this is what love demands :
the leap across the fence,
knowledge in the hands :

demands we should come clean
letting the sun bang down
where, stirred by love's long spoon.
our hearts go round.

That clarity is love,
knowledge that came to stay
when the long wind drove
the heart's bad fog away

was love, was the different thing
we saw in the banged light :
the world where colour is king
and love is a name for sight.

DON'T LET'S SPOIL IT ALL, I THOUGHT WE WERE GOING TO BE SUCH GOOD FRIENDS

For God's sake save me, or tell me my passion is of too awful a nature for you.—KEATS to FANNY BRAWNE, May 1820.

IT seems the poet made a bad mistake.
How could she know how awful passion was ?
The lesson is that breaking hearts must break.

Now sage biographers are sad because
She did not play the game they like to see.
The necessary did not come across.

But this was not a case of He and She.
It was a case of He himself alone.
No lock will open till you fetch the key.

The lesson is that dying men must groan ;
And poets groan in rhymes that please the ear.
But still it comes expensive, you must own.

So when she heard him speak out loud and clear
She had to disregard his tuneful cry :
She had to leave him choking in his fear.

The lesson is that dying hearts must die.

89

'LOVE is too young to know what conscience is,
Yet who knows not, conscience is born of love?'
It seems a meaning we could hardly miss.

Yet even such pellucid lines may prove
Unwilling to be readily construed ;
Their needle travels in a double groove.

For love we find both delicate and crude ;
And poets long ago began to ask
'Love rules the world, but is the world subdued?'

So understanding love is quite a task,
And Shakespeare was no more than being wise
In fitting out his statement with a mask ;

For love is always seen with bleary eyes
And conscience (meaning 'consciousness') defines
The fire that blazes in a gale of sighs.

But still for love the silly spirit pines
In searching for the logic of its dream,
In pacing endlessly those dark confines.

When love as germ invades the purple stream
It splashes round the veins and multiplies
Till objects of desire are what they seem ;

Then all creation wears a chic disguise,
And consciousness becomes a clever changer
Turning a punishment into a prize.

And so to every type love is a danger.
Some think it means no more than saying Yes,
And some turn canine when they reach the manger.

It seems a meaning we could hardly guess.

BIBLIOGRAPHY

The Laughing Hyena, by D. J. Enright. Routledge and Kegan Paul, 1953.

Bread rather than Blossoms, by D. J. Enright. Secker and Warburg, 1956.

Mixed Feelings, by John Wain. Reading University School of Art, 1951.

A Word Carved on a Sill, by John Wain. Routledge, 1956. (New York : St. Martin's Press, 1956.)

A Frame of Mind, by Kingsley Amis. Reading University School of Art, 1953.

A Case of Samples, by Kingsley Amis. Gollancz, 1956. (New York : Harcourt, Brace, 1957.)

Fighting Terms, by Thom Gunn. Fantasy Press, 1954.

The Sense of Movement, by Thom Gunn. Faber, 1957.

Poems, by Robert Conquest. Macmillan, 1955. (New York : St. Martin's Press, 1955.)

Poems, by Elizabeth Jennings. Fantasy Press, 1953.

A Way of Looking, by Elizabeth Jennings. André Deutsch, 1955. (New York : Rinehart, 1956.)

Brides of Reason, by Donald Davie. Fantasy Press, 1955.

The North Ship, by Philip Larkin. Fortune Press, 1945.

The Less Deceived, by Philip Larkin. Marvell Press, 1955.

The Minute, by John Holloway. Marvell Press, 1956.

And the Fantasy Press pamphlets: 'Fantasy Poets', Nos. 1, 16, 19, 21, 22 and 26 by Elizabeth Jennings, Thom Gunn, Donald Davie, Philip Larkin, Kingsley Amis and John Holloway respectively.

THE END

PRINTED BY R. & R. CLARK, LTD., EDINBURGH